Lucy Lessons

by Nancy Hadley, Ed. D.

Lucy Lessons
ISBN: 978-0-9833377-7-5
Copyright © 2014 by Nancy Hadley
Interior design and formatting by Grant Hill
Cover art, design and illustration by Sarah Stratton

Published by Garden Publishing Company
10403 US Highway 87 North
Sterling City, Texas 76951

This book or parts of this book may not be reproduced in any form, stored in a retrieval system, or transmitted in any form by any means - mechanical, electronic, photocopying, recording, or otherwise - without prior written permission by the author, except as provided by the United States of America copyright law.

Printed in the United States of America.

Garden Publishing Company

The American Standard Version of the Bible, © (ASV)
The King James Version of the Bible. © (KJV)
The Holy Bible, New International Version® (NIV®)
The New King James Version of the Bible, © (NKJV)
The New Living Translation of the Bible, © (NLT)

Dedication

I dedicate this work to my family - my loving husband, Jim; my precious daughter and son-in-law, Jennifer and John; my cherished son and daughter-in-law, Darby and Tonya; and my beloved mom, who was my greatest supporter.

Acknowledgements

I want to give special thanks to Sarah Stratton for the expressive illustrations of Lucy, which enhance the meaning of each lesson. Thank you for your excellent work.

Contents

Foreword	1
Introduction	5
Birth	11
A Life-Saving Drill	17
The Approach	27
Rest	33
Attention!	37
Obedience	43
Listening	49
Natural Ability	53
Control	59
Go!	63
Fetch!	67
Whoof!	73

Consequences	77
Vulnerability	81
Self-Absorbed	85
Too Contented?	89
Anxious	93
Whining	97
Stubborn Will	101
Missed Momoents	105
Keeping Watch	109
Expectancy	115
Zeal	121
Respect	125
Trapped	129
Breath	135
Perspective of Gifts	141
Short Leash	145
Time of Need	149

Anticipation	153
Thoroughness	159
Devotion	163
Stumbling	167
Epilogue	171
Don't Look At Me *by Sarah Stratton*	175

Foreword

Having read Nancy's previous book, *Finding Mom: A Daughter's Rite of Passage*, I was delighted when she brought me a copy of *Lucy Lessons* to look over. As a lover of Jesus and a lover of dogs, I took an immediate interest in the book's concept and the possibilities it opened to consider the ways a four-legged family member could reveal the very nature and depth of a believer's relationship with God. I was amazed.

In Lucy Lessons, Nancy has humbly opened up her heart, describing some stages in her life journey which happened to coincide with the life of a special friend named Lucy. In her emotionally raw and straightforward manner, Nancy welcomes us into her unique relationship with Lucy. She gives us many opportunities to laugh,

to ponder, to roll our eyes, and to praise God for His daily blessings. Most of all, Nancy offers a fresh invitation to press in to a deeper relationship with Jesus Christ.

Reading this book, I felt that not only had I been delightfully introduced to this wonderful little pet named Lucy, but I had also discovered so much about the way I interact with my creator. I recognized myself in several of Lucy's actions. I was reminded over and over that, though my Father in heaven may sometimes roll His eyes and chuckle at my shenanigans, He sees with a greater perspective and loves me with a magnificent love that allows Him to continue pursuing me, guiding me, enjoying me, and drawing me more and more into His great plans for my life.

It would be a mistake for any reader to pick up this book expecting a collection of silly stories about a dog. Instead, it is a testament to the simplicity and wonder of a walk with the King of kings. It is an invitation to recognize that deep spiritual mean-

ing is often tucked into everyday events. It is an opportunity to allow the Holy Spirit to examine our hearts and question our lives from the completely safe context of our own special place on Father God's lap.

Nancy has invited you to take a trip through her memories that will ultimately lead you closer to the throne of Grace. I pray you will accept her offer. As you read, I urge you to approach each Lucy Lesson in humility and allow the Holy Spirit to speak to you about each one. I encourage you to reflect in earnest, rejecting all condemnation but receiving afresh God's incredible love for you.

By the time you finish reading, I hope that Lucy will be as precious to you as she now is to me. You will quickly see why this perky little friend made such an impact on Nancy's life.

Funny isn't it – that our majestic God can choose to reveal Himself through a pet? His approach to our hearts is ever so

gracious, ever so playful, and ever so humble. May we all find grace to approach Him in such Lucy-like fashion.

Sincerely,

Kevin McSpadden

Introduction

Just after Christmas of 1995, my mom and I drove about two hours to pick up a schnauzer puppy. My kids had wanted a puppy for many years, but I held out, supposedly because I did not want to take on one more responsibility. However, in reality, I just did not want to become attached. Having owned beloved dogs as a child, I remembered all too well the heart-wrenching trauma of losing one.

Nevertheless, because I was feeling a little guilty about my plans to pursue a doctorate degree that would take me away from home weekly, I changed my mind. I rationalized that a dog would occupy our son, Darby, who was in fifth grade. Maybe a dog would provide him with company and possibly teach him about caring for a pet. However, I reasoned that we could not get Darby a dog without recognizing our older daughter, Jennifer's, long term desire for a pet. Even though Jennifer was a senior in high school headed for college and way beyond the pet stage, I concluded that we must give Jennifer the dog.

My husband, Jim, and I ignored the awkward timing and came to the conclusion that we could "give Jennifer" the puppy for her birthday, which was shortly after Christmas. This would be an add-on

to the car and other things we had already planned for her birthday. The strategy was for us to keep the dog for Jennifer until she had a place for it. In the meantime, Darby could take care of it for Jennifer and learn some responsibility in the process.

Excited to help, my mom searched the ads in the paper for a schnauzer since she had one herself. Because it was Christmas time, the puppy pickings were slim. Therefore, when mom located an out-of-town breeder who would meet us half way, we were out the door, even though it was a two hour journey.

I can remember the first time I saw Lucy in the box of squirming puppies. Mother and I picked her out as the cuddliest of the bunch, and I held her all the way home as mother drove. Although presented to Jennifer and carried on Darby's shoulder while Jennifer was off to college, from my perspective, Lucy was always my dog. I loved her from the first day I saw her. Never would I have imagined at that

time that God would choose to use Lucy to speak to me, that He would teach me about my nature through this precious pet, and that I would lose my beloved mother before I lost Lucy.

To me, *Lucy Lessons* is a priceless collection of the revelations I received while observing and reflecting on Lucy's behavior. It consists of journal entries I made over the years after observing and contemplating Lucy's actions. The journal itself contains more than these *Lucy Lessons*. It recounts an ever-changing relationship with God deepened by recording the thoughts He shared with me while I made a concerted effort to listen and reflect. *Lucy Lessons* is a part of that journal, relating conversations I had with God prompted by Lucy's behavior.

Lucy brought me great joy along with a perspective of how different her world was from mine. Hers was a simple world of dependency and devotion to her master, and it was her relationship to me

Lucy Lessons

that shed light on how I might improve my relationship with my master, Jesus Christ. I cherish these revelations because each one triggered a conversation with God and an exploration of His word. There are more questions than answers embedded in these discussions, and I hope these questions launch the reader into similar observations, examinations, and conversations.

Birth

Luke 2:11-12
For unto you is born this day in the city of David a Savior, which is Christ the Lord. And this shall be a sign unto you; Ye shall find the babe wrapped in swaddling clothes, lying in a manger.
KJV

Lucy Lessons

April 14th, 1996

Lucy Lessons started when Lucy was about 5 months old. I was taking her out to "do her business" in the backyard just before her doctor's appointment when a thought dropped with a thundering thud into my unsuspecting mind. In retrospect, I can see how the thought grew from a song by Kathy Matea on her Good News album, "Mary, Did You Know?" The melody was a gentle one, almost peaceful, but to me the lyrics delivered a message I could not shake. The song rhetorically asked Mary, the mother of Jesus, many questions, such as "Did you know that when you've kissed your little baby, you've kissed the face of God?" or "Mary did you know that your baby boy would someday walk on water?"

For some reason, I couldn't listen to the Matea song without tears. Of course from a mother's perspective, memories of cradling my own baby boy sentimentally tugged on my heart strings, but this was more. I seemed to be overwhelmed by

the thought of kissing the face of God as I would my own baby!

Why was I so moved by this version of the familiar story? I guess I never really thought about God subjecting Himself to the hands of imperfect human beings as a vulnerable infant. Because of His Mighty Love, He exposed Himself to being born as a baby to reach man, to talk to him, to restore relationship with him, and ultimately to shed His blood to save him.

I was considering the incredible fact that Jesus agreed to leave the glory of heaven to become a defenseless newborn as I rounded the corner of my house to catch up with Lucy. I looked down to see her gazing up at me with her trusting, loving, dark chocolate eyes. It struck me that in some ways what Jesus did would be like me choosing to be born a puppy so that I could communicate with Lucy in a language she understood.

Lucy hasn't got a clue. I talk to her,

Lucy Lessons

and she cocks her head from side to side, without a shred of comprehension. I know she doesn't have the capacity to grasp concepts on my level, and she's not built to understand as I do. But likewise, I have about as much appreciation of the immensity of God's world as Lucy has of mine.

Later that day, I loaded Lucy into the car for a trip to the vet to get her final puppy shot, and the comparison continued in my mind. She whimpered in anticipation when I put her in the car. I placed her in the floorboard and tried to comfort her. I told her to sit, and of course she immediately stood up and jumped up on the seat. As we drove she was tossed from side to side upon turning corners, and when we arrived at the vet, she was frantic. Lucy had no idea that what I was doing was for her own good. She had no perception of the view from my driver's seat.

What familiarity this scenario brought! Do I ignore God's warnings, or even try to understand them? Have I been

tossed from side to side in life with no idea that what I am going through could be used for my own good? Do I have any grasp of the Big Picture from God's perspective?

After years of walking with God, my mind still cannot comprehend the breadth of His love. It is inconceivable to me that God's own son would leave His throne and the glory of heaven to come to earth to communicate with us and show us how to work with His father to destroy the works of the devil. Would I give up my humanity to do something as unthinkable as being born a puppy's birth, live in a dog's world, and be slaughtered by ungrateful blue healers? Although flawed in the details, the comparison drove me deeper into thought.

I know that I am not equipped to understand the full extent of God's love, but I can take a few lessons from Lucy. When I return home from a long day, Lucy shivers with excitement. She almost jumps out of her skin at my touch. She licks my hand and entangles herself in my steps. She

Lucy Lessons

is blindly devoted to her master. Do I have that kind of excitement and anticipation when I meet my master in prayer? Am I anticipating His coming? Am I utterly devoted to my master? Do I entangle myself in His steps? Lucy enthusiastically runs ahead of me when I walk without a clue to my direction. Do I do the same without waiting for direction? She curls up at my feet, content to be near me. Am I content in His presence? I still have a limited capacity to understand my Lord's love, but Lucy helped me to catch a glimpse of it today.

A Life-Saving Drill

Isa 26:3-4
Thou wilt keep him in perfect peace, whose mind is stayed on thee: because he trusteth in thee. Trust ye in the LORD forever: for in the LORD JEHOVAH is everlasting strength:
KJV

May 29th, 1996

It was a beautiful, sunny day in May, and my son, Darby, was teaching Lucy how to swim to the steps of the pool in our backyard. Even though Lucy was only six months old at the time, Darby was throwing her in at various spots around the pool to see if she could get to the steps from any location around the pool. Since we all had school or work, Lucy would be left alone in the backyard during the day, and although she hated the water and would not go near it on her own, she must be able to swim to the steps of the pool in case she fell into the water. It must be an automatic reaction, and she must have the stamina to swim the length of the pool. Also, she must know which direction to swim to the steps.

At first, Darby was throwing Lucy into the pool and then calling to her as he stood by the steps. Lucy would come up from the water, and after she recovered from the shock of being thrown in, she would get her bearings or "center herself"

by following Darby's voice to the steps. Later, Darby threw her in to see if she could find the way herself instinctively without the direction of his voice. This was a life-saving drill for her, and it would take practice.

As I watched this take place, I felt like I was about to be thrown into a pool myself, although my pool was not a physical pool but a pool of despair. My mind raced to the fact that I would leaving in two days to begin summer school in Denton, Texas. I was frantically getting ready to embark on this adventure with God to pursue a doctorate degree. He was the one who directed me to do it, but I was very nervous. Just getting to the school would be a four and a half hour drive one-way, and I would be staying in a RV trailer park during the week while I was there. At the end of the week, I would drive home to pick up wifely and motherly duties. How would I manage all of that? I was certainly being thrown into deep waters just like Lucy. I knew I would need to be able to find my way to

the steps out if I wanted to survive. She was practicing swimming to safety, so maybe I should too!

But what would be my life-saving drill? How would I juggle all that I needed to juggle to complete this degree? How would I keep my focus centered on the important things before me, find the steps, and not drown in the details? How could I keep my composure? I knew God's word said to keep my mind focused on Him and rely on His strength. But what were the steps involved in actually doing that? Maybe I needed to practice some type of drill like Lucy was practicing so that I could keep myself afloat and remain peaceful through the process of the next couple of years?

In my mind I knew that God paved the way for me to go to school, so He would take care of me, but the thought of it overwhelmed me. Then I reasoned that just like Lucy was doing with Darby, I could follow God's voice to the steps of

my emotional pool by taking the time to listen to His voice. I just needed to center myself on His purpose, taking it one day at a time. I thought to myself, "That's how you eat an elephant, isn't it? You take one bite at a time!" The critical issue would be to keep "centered" during this experience because I KNEW I couldn't do this alone. How could I keep my balance and make "centering" the daily ritual it had to become? I needed to practice just like Lucy was doing, so that heading in the direction of the steps was an automatic response in my emergencies. Out of all the things I needed to do to prepare for this journey, this might be my most important one! But I was still unsure exactly what my drill would be.

God seemed to speak to me in His "still small voice" while I was contemplating. He said that first and foremost, I needed to check the intentions of my heart to make sure I was fully yielded and seeking His direction. It would be like the phrase in Isaiah, being "stayed on thee." I recalled the desperate times in my life when I had

to "center." In those times I desperately sought God throughout the entire day. God showed me that the last few days of anxiety had been "off center" for me, and I discerned a difference in the attitude of my heart. I had not been seeking Him throughout my day, minute by minute. I must talk to God in prayer in the morning and give Him my day, every day. When I forgot or got too busy, I lost my direction.

God was my "step" out of the pool of despair. He was my peace. Just as Lucy must find the steps of the pool no matter where she fell in, I must turn and head toward God in my heart when I got into deep waters. I could not get too busy to begin my day without direction and without giving my day to Him. God had provided for every detail of this experience and would continue to do so. I just needed to turn toward Him and rely on His provision. For me, "centering" seemed to be an exercise of the heart, where the majority of my conditioning had to take place. The first thing I must do in my life-saving drill was practice

the discipline of daily prayer to "center" and set my direction.

What could I do physically to "center?" Yesterday, I found myself tense all day, suffering through a headache no matter how much medicine I took. I remembered experiencing the rejuvenating physical healing of God's presence in my morning prayer. It washed over me like a refreshing rain, causing me to relax my facial muscles. I could literally feel the body tension dissipate. Perhaps I needed to take time to be in His presence and carry that presence throughout my busy day. I could hurry my hands, without being hurried in my spirit. Relaxing in His presence would help me center. Exercise would help too, creating the stamina I needed to complete my tasks and make it to the steps in my emotional pool. This aspect seemed trivial at first. Then I realized that if I diligently practiced, it could become automatic.

The most difficult aspect would be the mental steps. The mind, being separate

from the heart was the place I found my thoughts, not my intentions. I had to control the racing thoughts in my mind. Satan distracted and busied me in my mind. I had to use discernment as the gatekeeper of my mind. If my heart was headed toward the right direction, discernment would be easier. It took effort and conditioning to control my mind.

Also, I had to put the knowledge of God's word in my mind so he could illuminate the truths that applied to the moment. God could not illuminate His truths if knowledge of His word was not in my mind. He could not make connections clear or fit the puzzle together without some pieces with which to work.

Then a distinct visual popped in my mind. It was a vision of a board that described the birds native to Texas at the Nature Center in Ft. Davis State Park. I'm not sure the board is still there, but when I visited years ago, there were pictures of the birds on the board, and under each picture

was a little light bulb. Running along the left side of the board were all of the names of the birds with a slot by each name. There was a metal pencil attached with a string to the board. As soon as you touched the pencil to the slot by the name of the bird, the appropriate light under the picture of the bird illuminated. It was so clear to me that God would highlight familiar verses just like the lights under the pictures of the birds lit up at the touch of the pencil. I just needed those pictures of His word in my mind so he could highlight a truth when a situation arose. He would make the connections to fit my situation if I equipped my board with the pictures. I knew that I must begin a personal bible study. That seemed to be a critical missing element for me at this point. I must pack my study bible and chart a regular time in my new schedule.

As I was watching Lucy make her laps in the pool, my routine for "centering" emerged. Although this schedule might change, for the time it consisted of a morning prayer directing my day to God,

Lucy Lessons

relaxing in His healing presence, regular exercise, and a methodical personal bible study. By practicing this drill until it was automatic, if I fell into the pool of despair, I would be able to find my way to the steps that took me out of danger. Lucy mastered her drill, now I must master mine.

The Approach

Heb 4:16
Let us therefore come boldly unto the throne of grace, that we may obtain mercy, and find grace to help in time of need.
KJV

Lucy Lessons

2 Tim 1:7
For God hath not given us the spirit of fear; but of power, and of love, and of a sound mind.
KJV

October 11th, 1996

I am overwhelmed by my doctoral program in Denton. Fear knocks at my door after taking a major test. The result is uncertain. As I approach you, God, in my prayer time, my posture reminds me of Lucy. I would have never guessed that a puppy would teach me so much about our relationship. Lucy greets me with confidence, at times jumping up and wiggling with excitement. Other times she sees me coming and just rolls over, begging for me to rub her tummy. Then there are times when she approaches me with caution. She instinctively knows when something bad may happen, and at those times, she gets about 5 feet from me and crouches with her tail tucked. She creeps along slowly

with her belly dragging until she gets to my feet. Then she rolls over and begs for mercy, hoping I will respond positively.

    I find myself approaching You, God, in the same manner, sometimes bursting with excitement, sometimes begging for you to soothe me, and other times crouching timidly, approaching Your throne and seeking mercy. I know Lucy doesn't have a clue about my viewpoint as she cocks her head to one side with anticipation. I sometimes feel just as clueless about your perspectives as I strain to hear Your voice. It is beyond my comprehension that You would love me so much that You would send your son to live and die in my world to try to communicate in terms I can understand. I can't imagine subjecting myself to live and die in Lucy's world in order to communicate with her.

    You have provided for my needs today. I felt Your presence during my test, and now I want to jump in your lap to have You soothe my fear of the outcome. I just

Lucy Lessons

hope I am as appreciative as Lucy seems to be. I hope I can exhibit the enthusiasm she shows when I come into Your presence. Last night I was frantic when I couldn't get in touch with my husband, Jim, by phone. Where was he? Why didn't he answer? Did something happen to him?

All kinds of scenarios raced through my head while I sat in silence with fear gripping me. My mind drifted to a dark time when I got the call that my father's plane went down, and there were no survivors. I was alone then, and the silence was deafening. I just stood there sobbing in utter helplessness. That memory lurks in the corners of my mind sometimes when I sit alone as I did last night. I know how utterly fragile life is, and how quickly it is gone. Fearing the unknown triggers those memories, and at those times, I creep into your presence as Lucy does, knowing that bad things do happen.

However, Your Word tells me not to fear and assures me that I don't have

to creep into Your presence, but I can approach Your throne boldly to obtain mercy and grace in my time of need. There's no need to cringe at the unknown or anticipate misfortune because I have placed my trust in You, knowing You will see me through. You did not give me a spirit of fear. I know I can curl up in your provision at any time. Just like Lucy, I come to you in different ways at different times. Although my circumstances may dictate my posture as I come into Your presence, I can approach with confidence through the blood of Jesus.

Rest

Gen 2:2
And on the seventh day God ended his work which he had made; and he rested on the seventh day from all his work which he had made.
KJV

Matt 11:28
Come unto me, all ye that labor and are heavy laden, and I will give you rest.
KJV

February 4th, 1997

Nothing says rest like a sleeping puppy. Lucy is a little over a year old now and is curled up at my feet, unaware of what is going on in my hectic world as I continue to work on my doctorate. She is totally in my care. I have fed her, given her water, and now she is peacefully sleeping, content to be in my presence, even if I have had a rough day. She could pick any place in the house, but she prefers to be at my feet. It is funny how she moves with me around the house, and the moment I sit down, she plops down near me.

Lucy is unaware that I am weary from the day. She is oblivious to the fact that I have been running around all day, and now I am late for my meeting with

Lucy Lessons

You, God. I meant to get here earlier, but I just didn't get it done. I have such good intentions, but my flesh is weak. I do the things I do not want to do and do not do the things I do want to do, yet that does not affect Lucy at all. She is oblivious to the cares I entertain at my level. She has no idea what I do outside the confines of the house.

It occurs to me as I meet You here, God, that I have no idea what Your day has been like. Maybe I should ask how Your day has been! However when I consider that question, I wonder what days are like in eternity, much less what God does in His days. Since there is no darkness, there is probably no setting sun. How then are God's days marked? Since there is no time in eternity, how does one know the day has ended? Better yet, are there days in eternity? What would be the cue to lay down to rest? I know You, God, do not sleep, but do You rest? Your Word says You did on the seventh day after the work that You made.

Lucy Lessons

It is interesting that Your Word says that you will "give" me rest. I wonder what that means. I picture You passing out rest as my mom passed out hot rolls at the dinner table. Is rest a commodity? Is it tangible? What does rest look like from your viewpoint? My questions multiply as I contemplate. Questions aside, I know I am safe in the grip of Your love, no matter what Your day looked like. Help me to rest at Your feet every bit as peacefully as Lucy is resting at mine, unconcerned about my own cares and totally in Your care.

Attention!

1 Peter 5:8
Be sober, be watchful: your adversary the devil, as a roaring lion, walketh about, seeking whom he may devour,
ASV

Lucy Lessons

February 10th, 2003

I have long since finished my doctoral program, and Lucy is now over seven years old. Years have passed, and although I continue to journal, it has been a while since I thought about Lucy Lessons. However, today was the exception.

Sometimes when I sit in the recliner, I pick Lucy up and set her down at my side. She is more comfortable at my feet, but sometimes I just want her closer. So I place her by my side and insist she stay right there. As I push back in the chair to recline it, Lucy is hesitant. I don't know if it is the height of the chair that makes her uncomfortable or the fact that I am holding her in place that leaves her on edge. In any case, she eventually obeys and nestles in my chair with me. After a time, I can feel her relax and fall asleep.

However even if Lucy is in her deepest sleep, when I make the slightest movement in the chair, she bounds forth out of

the chair and hits the floor. In an instant she is completely alert, no matter how immersed in sleep she had previously been. She is ready for action as she awaits my next movement. It frustrates me sometimes because many times I am just moving around with no intention of getting up. At those times, I have to get out of the chair and move her back to her position or let her sleep at my feet. When I do get up, Lucy's focus is intently on my footsteps, and she awaits my lead. She tries to anticipate my direction and keenly watches as I walk for the slightest direction change. She doesn't run too far ahead. She keeps in step with my steps. If I stop, she stops and waits patiently for my next movement.

At these times I love the way she meekly peeks up at me through her eyebrows, trying to discern if she needs to respond. Her focus is intent on my feet and the direction of my movement as she snatches a quick glance at what lies ahead. I am amazed at how swiftly she goes from a sleep state to alertness, snapping to atten-

tion.

There are all kinds of similarities here, starting with my resistance to taking a seat at Your side, God, in a higher place. As I gently coaxed Lucy to stay by my side in the chair despite pushing the limits of her comfort zone, so you must persuade me to shed my flesh and come to higher ground when I am reluctant to do so. I need to train myself to attend to the things of the spirit and be willing to go there even amidst my busy day.

Then there is Lucy's response time to my movements. I hope I respond to Your movements, God, as quickly as Lucy does to mine. Lucy is completely focused on my whereabouts. She follows me around, delights in being close to me, and is highly sensitivity to any move I make. I want to be that in tuned to You, God. I want to react immediately and snap to attention. I want to move into action immediately at your call.

Lucy Lessons

Lucy has a single-minded focus on my behavior and is intently absorbed in determining the direction I am going. She wants to be right in step with me, not falling behind or running ahead. I want to be as captivated with You, God. My goal is to be as immersed in Your presence and as engaged with Your agenda as Lucy is with mine. Jesus was sent to us to destroy the works of the devil, and I know that is my mission as well. Jesus mirrored Your movements, Father, by only saying what You said and doing what He saw You do. Your word says that my adversary is pacing around just waiting for an opening to strike. Lucy seems ready to follow me in my mission. Will I be as ready as she is to follow You?

Obedience

Gal 5:18
For the flesh lusts against the Spirit, and the Spirit against the flesh; and these are contrary to one another, so that you do not do the things that you wish.
NKJV

Ps 111:10
Reverence for the LORD is the foundation of true wisdom. The rewards of wisdom come to all who obey him.
NLT

Ps 128:1-2
How happy are those who fear the LORD —all who follow his ways! You will enjoy the fruit of your labor. How happy you will be! How rich your life!
NLT

Prov 4:12-13
Carry out my instructions; don't forsake them. Guard them, for they will lead you to a fulfilled life.
NLT

March, 18th, 2003

It is not in Lucy's nature to hug, but I have trained her to cooperate. When I hug her, she obeys, but she is hesitant. She hangs her head, and you can tell she is un-

comfortable. She doesn't react naturally, so her movement is slowed and deliberate. For her, a hug is an act of controlled obedience. Her awkward reaction tickles me because it shows she merely tolerates the hug. She can't wait until it is over. What is natural to me is uncomfortably unnatural to her.

Nevertheless, Lucy's obedience pleases me. It is gratifying to me, not because of the quality of the hug or the reciprocation of the hug, but because of the simple fact that she does it. It is never her idea to hug, but she still tolerates it. She instinctively knows when I want a hug, because when I bid her to come to me, she hangs her head, tucks her tail, and slowly, after a period of refusal, creeps up to me just out of reach. I call her again and after hesitating, she moves a little bit closer. This goes on for quite a while. She peers out from under those bushy eyebrows as if to say, "do I have to?" Finally, she gets close enough for me to grab her. After we hug, she squirms as if to say, "enough is enough, and I am ready to get down."

Lucy Lessons

Sometimes I stand Lucy up on her hind legs and pull her toward me by her front legs. She tries to squat as I pull her towards me. It's funny to see her back side reluctantly following because if it could, it would readily detach. Lucy has learned to still herself because she doesn't have a choice, but I can tell the behavior is unnatural. She doesn't naturally give in to me; rather it is an obedient response.

I wonder if this is the way You feel, God, when I obediently respond to Your call. Does it tickle You, Lord, as it does me? When You call, do I hesitate like she does? How many times do I hang my head or pretend not to hear? How often is my response to You, an obedient response, suppressing my natural response? Your word says that the spirit and the flesh are contrary to one another. When I am angered, do I act deliberately instead of following what comes naturally? When You prod me to do something out of my comfort zone, do I respond no matter how awkward I feel? I should comply because your word is full of

reasons to obey, such as receiving wisdom, rewards, happiness, and fulfillment. How do You feel when I stubbornly sit down in offense when I know I should graciously forgive? Do You pull me towards You as I do Lucy, to coax me into doing You want me to do or what I know I should do? What do You feel when I duck my head and peer out from under my eyebrows at Your call to love my enemies? Do I squirm like Lucy does? May I get down now?

Listening

Matt 17:5
This is my Son, whom I love; with him I am well pleased. Listen to him!
NIV

Lucy Lessons

April 9th, 2003

This evening I was talking to Lucy, and she was straining to understand. She looked intently into my eyes, and as I spoke to her, my attention was drawn to the way her ears kept moving. They reminded me of radar antennas as they moved independently of one another to pick up different unseen frequencies. One ear would turn one way, and at the same time the other ear was turning in another direction. As she gazed into my eyes, it seemed like she was trying to "get a fix" on what I was saying. I was amazed at how her ears kept moving. She seemed to think if she could catch the sound in just the right way, maybe she could understand. I know she has a keen sense of hearing, so she was using that innate ability, her best sense, to try to make sense of what I was saying. I know that she will never understand, but her attempts warmed my heart.

I hope my attempts to listen to You, Lord, warm Your heart even though it

seems like I strain to understand what you are saying to me. Although I cannot turn my ears independently as Lucy does, her efforts make me want to earnestly use all my best faculties to "tune in" Your message. Your word tells me to listen to the words of Jesus. I will meditate on them more fervently. I will tune in to Holy Spirit so that He can help me comprehend Your message. The Holy Spirit inside me is indeed my best sense.

Natural Ability

1 Cor 7:7
*But each one has his own gift from God,
one in this manner and another in that.*
NKJV

October 18th, 2003

I was "jogging" in the pool on a Saturday morning, dressed in my resistance gear, getting some exercise when I thought to myself how much I loved being in the pool in October. The tree in the corner of the back yard provided a little shade along with a home for a pretty vocal mockingbird. Lucy loved to peer into the tree just in case she caught a glimpse of her noisy neighbor. One of her favorite hobbies was chasing the birds.

This morning Lucy was using another one of her best senses, her sense of smell, to check out the corner. Because I was in the pool, Lucy was slightly above eye level for me, and from this perspective, I was highly aware of her smallest movements. I saw her nostrils busily taking in the air around her. Even when she stood still, her nose remained in motion. I spoke to her rhetorically to ask her if she could see the clock on the wall by the house, and if she could tell me the time. Unaffected by

my distraction, she turned towards the tree and started taking in the smells at an even faster rate! I rarely had the opportunity to witness her from this close angle, and I was amazed at how rapidly and intricately she was sniffing. What was she after? What could she be sensing that caused her to employ this level of natural talent? I thought to myself, "You go girl!"

Despite Lucy's amazing display of sophisticated detective work, I lapsed back into thinking about my very busy week. As I treaded water in my pool, I felt like I had been spiritually treading water as well. I did not have the time, or rather I did not make the time for reading my bible or for journaling. Uncomfortable with that thought, my mind wandered to the lyrics from a song that I was trying to remember. It seems that lately I have been immersed in many new, inspiring Christian songs, and although I was not making progress in study, I had been lost in worship. Many of the phrases that I hear in those songs seem to hit me like surprise punches, creating vi-

sual images that captivate my mind. Sometimes one image will trigger another, and before I know it, a bigger picture emerges. It occurred to me that I think a lot in pictures.

The phrases I tried to remember from the song were something like "You bring me to a place above the crowds" followed by "I can see other faithful believers." As the visuals from those two phrases collided, an epiphany popped out in my mind's eye. I could see people rising out of my pool, being lifted on what seemed like clear pedestals. The water represented the busyness and chaos below, and the people were faithful believers being lifted above it all. I smiled to myself as I somehow knew they saw me as I saw them. From the vision, I understood that Jesus really does lift us out of our circumstances to a peaceful place where His presence resides. I imagined that in that place, we can not only see Jesus, but other believers as well. That made me smile!

Lucy Lessons

It occurred to me that You, Lord, often speak to me through the lyrics of songs. When I stop to allow you to combine the visual images I get from the songs, I can often see a bigger picture. Because I have immersed myself in worship songs lately, that is what You have used to speak to me today.

Lucy takes in all the smells around her and gleans understanding from one of her strengths, her keen sense of smell. One of my strengths seems to be a visual sense. Although I am not sure about the full meaning of this particular insight, I am excited about how it came together. I am encouraged by knowing that you built me this way, and that you will use what you gave me, my natural abilities, to speak to me.

Now I must immerse myself in Your Word. Then You can use the visuals I get from it to create more insight for me. I look forward to those epiphanies. Lucy has her smells to discern; I have my pictures. Your

word tells me that each one has his own gift. I am good with that.

Control

Matt 10:39
He who finds his life will lose it, and he who loses his life for My sake will find it.
NKJV

Lucy Lessons

October 31st, 2003

Today I am reminded of a Lucy Lesson about control – control of the bone. At times Lucy will bring me her bone to seemingly play catch, but she really has no intention of playing catch. It's really tug-of-war that she has in mind, and she turns passionate about it. She presents the bone to me as if to hand it to me. However, when I take hold of the bone, she locks her jaw and digs in. Her demeanor changes drastically, and she begins to growl and clench her teeth. As I tug, the pitch in her growl changes to a ferocious level. She throws her whole body into the effort, carefully positioning herself to leverage her weight. She actually pulls from her toes through her entire hind quarters, lowering her center of gravity. At times I have even lifted her high off the ground as she hangs on to the bone with her clenched jaw. She will not let go! The battle quickly changes from a game to a war complete with an aggressive growl.

Do I do the same with control of my

life, Lord? Do I seemingly hand it to You then I hold on for dear life? Your word says that he who finds his life loses it, and he who loses it for Your sake finds it. I guess "finding and losing" is talking about control, and I need to let go. As you tug to gain control and I feel like I am losing it, do I dig in and fiercely hang on with clenched determination? If only I could only play catch with you! I could bring you my life, and you could toss it out in the direction You want me to go. Racing in that direction, I would then bring the control back to you for further direction. Instead I offer You control then the tug of war ensues. Is that where the enemy gets me off track? Is that where he gets me to operate in my flesh when I think I know best? I am picturing myself in some situations hanging in mid-air from the bone with my jaw locked on to my way. Oh to learn from this Lucy Lesson!

Go!

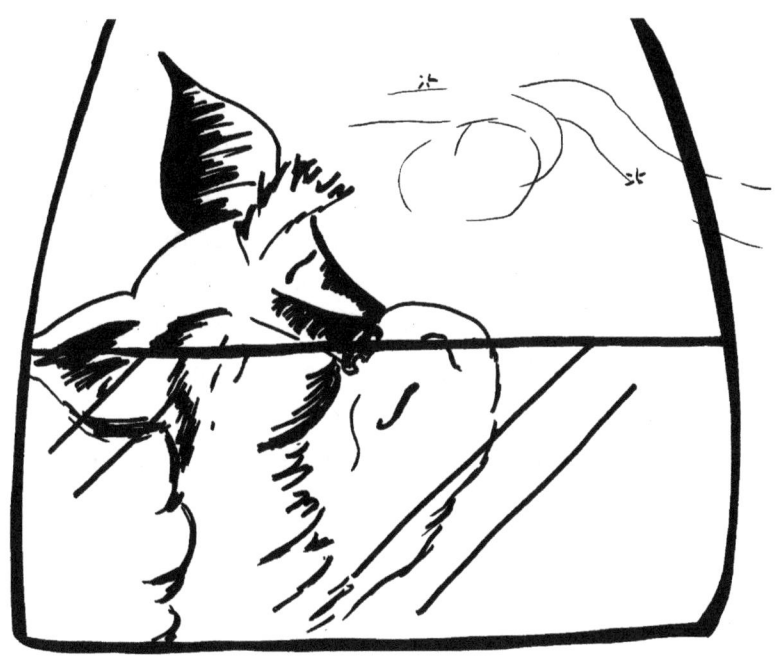

James 4:14-15
For what is your life? It is even a vapor that appears for a little time and then vanishes away. Instead you ought to say,"If the Lord wills, we shall live and do this or that."
NKJV

January 6th, 2004

I took Lucy in the car today to run errands. She was so excited to "go." As I told her she could go, her ears perked up in anticipation. She gazed at me intently, straining her ears to try to decipher my words. She let out a squeal at the possibility. I took her outside to "empty her tank" before the trip. She knew that was a prerequisite. After completing her "business" she raced to the door and jumped to the height of the door knob squealing again in expectation. I couldn't believe she jumped that high! After letting her in the car, I felt her excitement.

When in the car, Lucy raced from one window to the other in the backseat, pausing shortly at each window. During the pause, she glared at me to remind me how the window was supposed to be. A cracked window was everything to her. The destination of the trip was minor in comparison to the joy of an open window during the ride. She was definitely a proponent

of "smelling the roses" along the way. Of course the wind in her face rivaled in importance to all the smells she took in along the way. When the wind got too intense, she backed off, ran to the other window, and sneezed all over the window. Then she was back for more.

It really didn't matter where we went; it only mattered how – with or without an open window. Of course the value I placed on the trip along with my experience during the trip was totally different. I wondered if the same applied to You and me, God. What would I miss in my adventure through my time on earth?

I know life is a journey, and my final destination will be with you in eternity. Your word says that my life in this world is just a vapor, and then it vanishes. You, God, are not bound by time, nor are You as interested in time as I am. Just as I do not relate to the open window sensations or pleasures for Lucy, You must not relate to my obsessions with time, being on time, or running out of time. I am not sure I could relate to Lucy about my perspective on our trip together. She would never understand, just as I often miss Your point on our trip through time together. However, You did send Your son to clarify Your point. I must study more on His words and call on Holy Spirit to translate. Father, thank you for both Jesus and the Holy Spirit to help me on my journey until I get to be with You in eternity. Sometimes I still miss the point, but at least I have a shot at understanding more with what you have given me. I do love You, God.

Fetch!

Ps 62:5
My soul, wait silently for God alone, For my expectation is from Him.
NKJV

Lucy Lessons

Prov 12:15
*The way of a fool is right in his own eyes;
But he that is wise hearkeneth unto
counsel.*
ASV

January 21st, 2004

Lucy's agenda is always the same. She has one game that she likes to play, no matter what the toy is, and her game is tug-of-war. In addition, she likes to play on her terms. However, I have been trying to shape her behavior so that she will play fetch, and her reaction has been interesting.

After Lucy prances in with her toy, she plops it down just out of my reach. It amazes me that she places it close but out of my reach. I would think if she wanted me to play, she would place it within my reach, but I guess somehow her instinct is to draw me closer to her controlled space. I wait a while before I attempt to pick it

up, as she sits tentatively, anticipating my participation. When I go for the toy, she often beats me in grabbing it. A short tug-of-war ensues. She really wants me to play, so when she thinks I am going to release it, she has learned to let up briefly. If she does not let go, I drop my end. Then she brings the toy back to tempt me into the game again. When I refuse to play, she will bring the toy closer and sit with the toy in her mouth. After I show no interest, she reluctantly releases the toy. If I wait, she will even back away from the toy. She watches for my movements and lunges for the toy when I grab it. She really prefers tug-of war and is persistent in her efforts to play with me.

Finally I prevail in determining the game we will play, secure the toy and hold it up. Lucy's body becomes rigid with anxious anticipation. Watching me intently, Lucy leaps in the direction she thinks I will throw and races to the anticipated landing spot, never looking back. When she arrives, her eyes dart back to me. She can hardly

wait for me to throw the toy. She jumps gleefully to catch the toy when I do throw it. Every time she dutifully retrieves it but again, she places it just out of my reach. I think to myself, "Will she ever learn this simple game? Other dogs play this game well, so why can't she?" Once again, I must grab the toy with a quick movement for the game to continue. If I am successful, all goes well as long as this predictable process is repeated.

However, sometimes instead of throwing the toy to Lucy in the spot she has picked out, I throw the bone in the opposite direction. After she races to her preferred spot, she turns to look at me, and when I throw the toy, she sits frozen in disbelief with a confused look on her face. The game is often over when I surprise her. She does run to pick it up, but her interest in the game fades.

This behavior creates many questions, God. Your word says to wait silently for You and get my directions and expecta-

tions from you. How often do I sit at Your feet, Precious Lord, thinking I am waiting for Your lead, but the truth is that I have my preferred activities, and I want You to play my game on my terms? How often do I situate myself just out of Your reach, waiting for Your rescue? Why is it that I revert to my instincts and persist in the tug-of-war game when You want to send me in the direction of Your choice? I fool myself into thinking I am obediently waiting for Your lead, but I am hanging on to my own agenda. Is my preferred game tug-of-war no matter what? When will I learn to submit completely, drop my expectation, and truly be ready for Your call, Your terms, Your way?

Then I wonder how I react when You surprise me with a miss-direction. I am eager to run ahead in the direction I want to go, and I am confused when I look back to see my toy thrown in the opposite direction. Do I lose interest, and does my enthusiasm to race in the direction You chose for me fade as well? Your word says that a fool

Lucy Lessons

has it his own way and ignores counsel. Let me sit at Your feet completely free of my own agenda and race in whatever direction You choose. Better yet, let me wait for the direction and not race ahead. Let me lose my expectations and be open to Yours. Let me have faith in Your choices for me. Lucy is slow to learn the game; let me be quicker. I love Lucy. She reveals so much about my nature.

Whoof!

Rom 7:15-16
I don't understand myself at all, for I really want to do what is right, but I don't do it. Instead, I do the very thing I hate.
NLT

Lucy Lessons

January 21st, 2004

There is something Lucy cannot control, despite both her efforts and ours: barking at the doorbell. Lucy literally cannot control it. We have tried every behavioral tactic to get her to stop barking, including spraying water in her face. Jim has thrown her in the pool when she barks at the doorbell, a fate she detests, but no matter what, Lucy cannot control the "whoof" that comes out of her mouth. When she was younger she would burst into a vocal tirade, but as the years have gone by she has calmed down a bit. She knows she is not supposed to bark, and at times she hangs her head and tucks her tail after the "whoof" comes out. One time she even cowered and retreated to a back room after her response. Even when she is in my lap and I am holding her mouth shut, the "whoof" comes out. Lucy knows better, but her nature is to bark, so that is what she does.

I know my tendencies are the same

way. In Your word, Paul talks about the pattern of not doing what he wants to do and doing what he hates. The things I do not want to do, I sometimes do anyway. The things I want to do, I often do not get around to doing. There is something in my nature that is so hard to break. It takes all the control I can muster to fight a triggered response. Sometimes I am successful at suppressing it, and then other times, the "whoof" just comes out. I am so thankful that You are a God of love and grace so that in those times I can repent for my actions, and Your forgiveness covers me.

Consequences

Prov 22:3
*A prudent person foresees the danger
ahead and takes precautions; the simpleton
goes blindly on and suffers the
consequences.*
NLT

January 21st, 2004

This is the third Lucy Lesson of the day which must be a record! Lucy loves to bust through the bathroom door when I am taking a bath. However, she has come to know the consequences of her actions. Immediately after she bursts through the door, I reach out and push the door shut. She can't open the door from the inside, and she becomes trapped. I can see her face when she sees the door close. It's like an "Uh oh!" She goes immediately to the door and tries to open it with her nose. When unsuccessful, she comes to me, circles around as if to say, "The door is closed; please open it." Then she goes back to the door and peers at it. When that doesn't work, she again circles by me as if to say more emphatically, "Please open the door!" I tell her to sit down to wait for my timing, but she impatiently paces, peering at the closed door.

I'm sure I do the same thing when I face the consequences of my actions. I

look for ways around the closed door and pray for mercy and a way out. You patiently remind me that it will be in Your timing, but until then, I must wait. You would think Lucy would learn her lesson and not bust through the door. The instant she sees the door close behind her she knows she is trapped by the consequences of her actions, but it does not stop her from busting through the door. I too have a hard time learning from past experiences. I find myself behind that same door trapped in familiar consequences. You would think I would learn as well. Your word says that a simpleton goes blindly on and suffers the consequences. A simpleton is ignorant or silly. Am I a simpleton at times?

Vulnerability

Prov 29:25
Fearing people is a dangerous trap, but to trust the LORD means safety.
NLT

February 9th, 2004

Lucy shows me what vulnerability looks like. As I am taking off my shoes, she submissively comes close to where I am sitting and rolls over on her back, exposing her vulnerable underside. Inevitably, I rub her belly with my foot, and she groans her approval.

As I rub Lucy's belly, it occurs to me how easy it would be for me to crush her from this vantage point. She playfully nudges my foot with her feet, but she allows me to rub even her tender tummy area. Her ribs offer no protection to this area, yet she opens up this exposed area to the touch of my foot. Sometimes she seems reluctant, but experience tells her that she can trust me. Her mouth brushes against my foot, and I feel the sharpness of her teeth. At any moment they could come to her defense, but her gestures are controlled. She must work at letting her defenses down and not yielding to her natural instincts to protect herself. I can tell the reward is satisfying by

her expressive groans.

I wonder if I am as instinctively guarded. Your word, Lord, tells me that fearing people is a dangerous trap, and that I should trust the Lord because that brings me safety. I too must work at lowering my defenses with You, particularly when my weakest areas are exposed. I am not sure I am as eager to volunteer for vulnerability or if I can control my protective instincts long enough to reap the rewards. How much more would You, my Lord, protect my private concerns. Experience assures me of Your tender care, yet I'm not sure I am as eager to lay down my defenses. I cannot resist Lucy when she comes to me and rolls over. I always give her the intimate moment she craves. You have never disappointed me either.

Self-Absorbed

Prov 18:2
*A fool hath no delight in understanding,
But only that his heart may reveal itself.*
ASV

June 8th, 2004

Lucy and I were out of sync this morning. We had different agendas, and she was immersed in hers. I let her out to do her morning business while I began my workout. Normally, after a short time, she comes to the door, and I let her in to be with me during my exercise time. She usually brings me a toy while I am on the floor to play a brief but enthusiastic game of tug-of-war, which is her absolute favorite.

Today Lucy lingered too long and missed her opportunity to play. After exercising, I let her in and sat down to be with the Lord for a few minutes. By then, Lucy was ready to play. However, it was too late then; I had moved on to other things. Normally, she enjoys sitting next to me during this time, and because she couldn't settle down, she missed that as well. Lucy not only missed the opportunity to play during my exercise time, but she also missed the closeness she relishes during my quiet time.

Lucy Lessons

Later, I left the door cracked during my bath which serves as an invitation for Lucy to open the door and join me for a one-on-one conversation. However, she knows once she enters, the door closes behind her, and she is also my captive. Today she chose to open the door but not cross the threshold. I could tell from her demeanor she had other plans. I heard her gleeful groans as she scratched her back while wallowing on the carpet in the bedroom. It seemed like our schedules just didn't jive this morning, as Lucy chose not to comply with my plans for interacting with her.

Father, help me in my choices today. Remove my self-centeredness. Help me to seize the opportunities You provide and adjust my agenda to Yours. Your word tells me that a fool only wants "his way." Lucy chose a different path today, and we didn't connect. My priority is to connect with You today and to not be a fool. Expand my awareness of Your plans for interacting with me.

Too Contented?

Prov 6:8-9
*But you, lazybones, how long will you
sleep? When will you wake up?*
NLT

Eph 5:14
*Awake, O sleeper, rise up from the dead,
and Christ will give you light.*
NLT

June 20th, 2004

I left the door to the bathroom cracked again this morning, inviting Lucy to come in to visit. My intention was to enjoy her company while I took my bath. In the bath, I am almost at eye level with her, and I enjoy looking into her eyes and watching her reactions. Sure enough she burst through the door. I pushed the door closed behind her, and she circled the room checking out the territory. She gave me a quick glance and sniff, and then I invited her to sit close so that I could talk to her.

However, today Lucy was restless. Refusing my invitation, she stood peering at the door. I knew her intentions were to leave. Again I invited her to sit and visit, coaxing her closer. Despite my pleas, she

circled impatiently and resumed her pose at the door. Then Lucy began to scratch at the door. On several occasions she has been able to open the door with a combination scratch with her paw and nose nudge. Today she succeeded. After my bath I found Lucy contently curled up in her favorite spot on the bedroom carpet.

How often am I restless in Your presence, Lord, preoccupied with my own agenda and eager to get on with my day? How often do I snub your invitation to visit and gaze into Your eyes? Just this morning I awoke early and began praying. It wasn't long before I had dropped back off to sleep, missing the opportunity to hear Your voice. What a waste! Your word tells me to awake to receive the light. I don't want to be a lazybones. Help me not to be content in my own space, but to actively seek a spot close to you.

Anxious

Phil 4:6-7
Be anxious for nothing, but in everything by prayer and supplication, with thanksgiving, let your requests be made known to God; and the peace of God, which surpasses all understanding, will guard your hearts and minds through Christ Jesus.
NKJV

June 22th, 2004

Lucy joined me this morning during my bath. I was surprised when she busted through the door. She didn't even seem too upset when I closed the door behind her. She circled, sniffed, and sat down on the rug. As I began talking to her, she sat down and seemed to be satisfied. However, her contentment lasted for only a minute. Instead of enjoying the moment, she jumped up and resumed her impatient pose, staring at the door. I told her I would open it soon enough and tried to coax her into relaxing and enjoying the company. She persistently stood at the door in an insistent stance for the entire time.

Father, Your word tells me to be anxious for nothing. How much precious time have I wasted in tense, anticipation? How quickly I lose my peace! I guess I am anxiously waiting at the door just like Lucy, especially when it comes to some resolution with my mother. Earlier this year she had a stroke after heart surgery and be-

came paralyzed on the right side, unable to speak. My heart keeps breaking over and over, and each time the break feels new. I am anxiously waiting for the time when both Mother and I will be released from this agony. I find myself peering at a closed door, straining to hear the reason for this entrapment, and anticipating an end to the dilemma.

Do I just enjoy the company with my mom? Even though she cannot speak, I have noticed the pleasure in holding her hand, trading squeezes in silence, unencumbered with conversation. I guess the meaning of an emotion-packed squeeze of the hand is unmistakable communication of love. Our hugs convey the same sentiment. I know one day I will yearn for just one more hug and just one more moment. I must not peer impatiently into the future looking for an end that is not under my control. As painful as her situation is, my time with her is still intimacy shared between mother and daughter. I do cherish the time, and I trust you, Lord, with this

Lucy Lessons

situation. Increase my faith so that I am content with Your timing, which I know is perfect. Help me to enjoy every moment with not only Mother but with You and be truly anxious for nothing!

Whining

John 6:43
Murmur not among yourselves.
KJV

Lucy Lessons

January 6th, 2005

It was a busy morning for me. Many agenda items were on my mind as I drew the bath water. I left the door cracked for Lucy but didn't expect her. She hadn't connected with me in the bathroom in a while, and she wasn't in the vicinity. I didn't plan to linger, but I would have enjoyed a couple of moments with Lucy had she chosen to join me.

Lucy startled me when she burst in, but I quickly pushed the door closed behind her to capture her. She seemed particularly focused on her agenda, as was I. She went immediately to the door and stared intently with her head ducked. Her intent was clear and irritating to me. She hadn't even come close to sniff my vicinity. She did not seem interested at all in spending even a minute in my presence. Her posture became increasingly rigid, which felt uncomfortable for me. I beckoned her to come close and sit for a moment. She impatiently came near, huffed, and then re-

turned to the door.

I responded to Lucy, "Open the door if you want out" in the tone that encouraged her action. She pawed at the door in response. When unsuccessful she shook to indicate she wanted a reply. Then to raise the level of concern, she began her signature, breathy, almost inaudible whine that she had perfected in recent months. It sounds like a rush of air forced through her vocal chords just shy of full vibration, and it was her way of communicating her desires.

Lucy had made the few moments I had to spend uncomfortable, and I found myself wanting her to succeed in escaping. Her desires were loud and clear, and the noise disrupted the fleeting moments of peace I had to spend. I responded again with and emphatic "Open the door!" She scratched vigorously again, and this time she succeeded. I pushed the door closed behind her in relief.

Lucy Lessons

It occurred to me how often I enter Your presence, God, with the same attitude and purpose. Lately I have been trying to hear Your voice as a way of life. In doing so I am trying to listen without an agenda. I am trying to hear whatever You want to say to me. This morning Lucy reminded me how different it is to be in someone's company with an agenda. Even posture speaks loudly and often irritatingly. Your word, Lord tells me not to murmur. The selfish whine of the flesh crowds out any two way communication and tends to suffocate the other party. I didn't like to be in Lucy's company this morning. She had no receptive quality in her countenance, and today was all about her desires. I don't want to enter Your presence making this same mistake!

Stubborn Will

Ps 139:23-24
Search me, O God, and know my heart: try me, and know my thoughts; And see if there be any wicked way in me, and lead me in the way everlasting.
ASV

Prov 16:9
A man's heart deviseth his way: but the LORD directeth his steps.
KJV

January 24th, 2005

I was sitting on the floor tonight when Lucy approached me with her toy. She had tug-of-war in mind as she coaxed me into her game. I grabbed the toy and hung on for a little longer than usual. My position on the floor brought me closer to eye level with her. It was her eyes that struck me as we commenced the game. There was a definite change from her usual expression as the game ensued. She tugged with her whole body, and her growl reached a frenzied pitch. Her lip curled up over her clenched teeth, and then the twinkle in her eyes glazed over with savage intensity. I didn't recognize her in this ferocious state.

Then a noise from the other room broke the spell. Lucy froze for a moment,

and the eyes I knew to be Lucy's returned for a split second. But I held on to the toy, and she snapped back into the vicious glare. Amazed at the total transformation, I continued my study. I got as close as I dared, and with a persistent grip on the toy, I softened my voice to coax the twinkle back in her eyes. She paused for a moment, but quickly lapsed back into the cold stare. I really didn't like this stranger and quickly lost interest in the game. Her primal nature and determination to win were clearly evident in her eyes, turning her from a familiar friend to an unrecognizable foe.

I hope my self-determination doesn't make me as repulsive to You, God, as Lucy was to me at that moment. I hope I am more pliable than she was. As Your word says, I want you to search me and remove all that is not of You. I don't want my heart to devise my ways; rather I want You to direct my steps. I dropped my hold on the toy, which broke the trance on Lucy. Lucy persisted in her grip for quite a while. I hope I have learned to lay down my will

more quickly and follow Yours. During the times I display my ugly side, I am glad You look at the Jesus in me instead of my stubborn will. That would be the only way You could stand the sight of me!

Missed Moments

James 4:8
Draw near to God and He will draw near to you.
NKJV

Lucy Lessons

March 4th, 2005

I was in the dressing room this morning when Lucy nudged the door open. I turned to welcome her, and saw that she was crouched just outside the door. Usually she nudges the door open on her way through it, but today she held her ground outside the door. I beckoned her in, and she refused. It was a timid refusal, as if to ask permission to stay outside. Most of the time I close the door behind her, and I sensed she really didn't want to be trapped. She wanted to be in my presence but not confined. I would have spent some time focusing on her, but she missed her chance. Instead she settled a few feet away, and we missed those moments together. I called her again, and she peered up through her eyebrows shrinking lower. I reassured her and summoned her again. She obeyed tentatively as I rewarded her obedience with loving strokes. Then she returned to her position outside the door.

How often do I settle in my own

space when I could be in the presence of my master? Am I afraid of God's terms for intimacy? Do I take every opportunity provided to me to just be in His presence? How many times am I reluctant to abandon my will to enjoy God's perfect love? Am I willing to wait for the answers to my petitions? Do I trust Him completely with my circumstances? El Elyon, the God Most High, patiently waits for me to join Him. Can I sit quietly in His presence? The word says that if I draw near to you, Lord, you will in turn draw near to me. Will I nudge the door open and charge through the door, or will I crouch at the doorway, holding on to my control? I don't want to miss the loving strokes or tender moments, but am I willing to release control to enjoy the feast? Lucy made her choice. I want to choose differently.

Keeping Watch

Eph 6:12-18
For our struggle is not against flesh and blood, but against the rulers, against the authorities, against the powers of this dark world and against the spiritual forces of evil in the heavenly realms. Therefore put on the full armor of God, so that when the day of evil comes, you may be able to stand your ground, and after you have done everything, to stand...

... Stand firm then, with the belt of truth buckled around your waist, with the breastplate of righteousness in place, and with your feet fitted with the readiness that comes from the gospel of peace. In addition to all this, take up the shield of faith, with which you can extinguish all the flaming arrows of the evil one. Take the helmet of salvation and the sword of the Spirit, which is the word of God. And pray in the Spirit on all occasions with all kinds of prayers and requests. With this in mind, be alert and always keep on praying for all the saints. NIV

2 Cor 10:3-6
For though we live in the world, we do not wage war as the world does. The weapons we fight with are not the weapons of the world. On the contrary, they have divine power to demolish strongholds. We demolish arguments and every pretension that sets itself up against the knowledge of God, and we take captive every thought to make it obedient to Christ. NIV

Lucy Lessons

August 23rd, 2005

Animals have a keen sense of their surroundings. They understand the dangers of their habitat and continually evaluate approaching intrusions. My morning walk takes me by a field where the deer, in alert stance, appraise my intentions. The slightest movement in their direction sends them running. Further along my path, I approach a tree that is often filled with hundreds of chattering birds. As I pass under the tree, there is an immediate silence as the birds evaluate the threat and anticipate flight.

Likewise, Lucy often posts herself at the doorway of the room and utters a low "whoof" even during her nap to signal outside movement or sounds that are undetectable to me. I think she is asleep, but her keen sense of hearing keeps her intensely aware of her surroundings. Many times after she issues her warning, I go to the window and see a cat walking by or someone on a walk. I am amazed at her ability to

hear and the accuracy of her forewarning.

Ephesians 6:12 warns us of the nature of our battles and what we are truly up against. It clearly states that we struggle not against the flesh and blood that we see but the spiritual forces we cannot see. Those forces are described with words like "authorities" and "powers" from a dark world in heavenly places. To battle in this kind of war, the passage tells us to put on an extensive set of armor so we can stand. It goes on to say that after we do everything we can do, we must stand again. For a third time it warns us to stand firm. That is a lot of standing and contending against a force we cannot see. The passage finally tells us to pray and be alert at all times.

Second Corinthians 10:3 states, "For though we live in the world, we do not wage war as the world does." It goes on to describe the dangers that invade the mind in a spiritual conflict I largely ignore. It is in the unseen world that this battle takes place. I could learn a lesson from the wisdom of

animal instinct to make myself aware of the hostile forces around me which invade my innermost places. I need to post myself at the entrance of my mind to evaluate each approaching thought. As 2 Corinthians 10:5 states, I must "take captive every thought and make it obedient to Christ." Lucy keeps watch even in her sleep. Am I as ready as she is, or am I asleep during my watch? Am I focusing on what I can see or on what I cannot see? Am I even trying to understand the nature of the battle? Lucy is extremely aware of her surroundings. Do I have a clue about mine?

Expectancy

Matt 7:11-12
If you, then, though you are evil, know how to give good gifts to your children, how much more will your Father in heaven give good gifts to those who ask him!
NIV

Isa 53:5
But He was wounded for our transgressions, He was bruised for our iniquities; the chastisement for our peace was upon Him, and by His stripes we are healed.
NKJV

September 26th, 2005

    I was making my lunch this morning and couldn't help but notice Lucy's intent gaze. She was perched close by in a polite pose. Her ears were at attention, and her face was full of anticipation. She waited, quietly restraining her hope. She perked up when I glanced her way, then settled in again when I continued my task. She is so cute in this stance that it was hard not to reward her diligence. I was overcome with compassion and directed my attention her way. Again her expectancy rose. At that point there was no way I would have disappointed her. I headed for the treats, applauding her winning ways.

Lucy Lessons

Lucy has it down, the joyful anticipation of something good. Her body language exudes anticipation. Her ears are at attention, her eyes sparkle, her breath is short, her posture is erect, and her gaze is intent. She is able to move instantly in reaction to the slightest change of my position. She constantly displays this expectancy when I am in the kitchen, despite occasions that have produced no fruit for her. I love to see her enthusiastic eagerness for what I might provide. I delight in rewarding her hope.

What was clear to me this morning was that my satisfaction in responding to Lucy is only an inkling of God's pleasure in granting the desires of my faith. But this morning my thoughts went a little further. What am I sitting and waiting for in faith? What is my understanding of the possibilities? What do I believe are my promises? Isaiah 53:5 says, "But He (Jesus) was wounded for our transgressions, He was bruised for our iniquities; the chastisement for our peace was upon Him, and by

His stripes we are healed." Let me get that straight. Jesus paid the full price for me to have not only freedom from sin, but freedom from the things that plague me in life and freedom from disease. These are some of my promises because of my covenant with Jesus. In one supernatural event, He demolished the works of Satan, winning my freedom over not just sin, but over torment and disease. Therefore if there is any area of my life where I am not sitting at the God's feet with joyful anticipation of something good, then that may be an area that is influenced by the devil.

I must keep the picture of Lucy eagerly awaiting what I will do as a model for my behavior before the Lord. I rewarded Lucy with a treat. How much more will my Father honor my faith? How much more will He reward my eager hopes as I sit at His feet gazing with anticipation at Him? His word assures me that He does give good gifts, and that Jesus paid the price for the things I have done wrong. God's love is immeasurable, and His resources have

no end. How He must love the sight of His children quietly awaiting His attentions! I can take a lesson from Lucy's devoted demeanor. Her hope won me over. How much more will mine win my Father? I just need to have a clear understanding of His promises so that I can hope for what was intended for me.

Zeal

Isa 9:7
The zeal of the Lord of hosts will perform this.
NKJV

Cor 12:9

And He said to me, "My grace is sufficient for you, for My strength is made perfect in weakness."
NKJV

October 10th, 2005

It was a rainy morning. The grass was wet, so Lucy's feet and underside were drenched after attending to her morning business. She desperately wanted to come inside, and she enthusiastically pursued her goal by jumping and dancing on her hind legs. I retrieved a towel to dry her off and began working on the task. She failed to recognize the importance of this task as it related to her goal, so she fought my efforts. She kept pulling away each foot as I fought to dry it off, so I finally picked her up. She continued to squirm, unaware that her exuberance was delaying the realization of her objective. In her zeal, she was actually working against her goal. Finally she relaxed and allowed me to complete the task.

How often do I work passionately in my own strength, unknowingly preventing my own progress? Does my zeal keep me from the power and direction God wants to provide? How do I relax and press into His strength? How do I lean on His understanding, not my own? How do I let His zeal accomplish my tasks?

Later I led Lucy to her water, bidding her to take a drink. She was trying to clear her throat after a dry treat, and she needed water. She didn't take the drink because she thought I was going to give her another treat. She didn't follow my lead, missing the refreshment of the water she needed.

I do not want to miss the treats or refreshments, nor do I want to delay my progress in my eagerness. Teach me, Lord, to lean on You, on your strength and understanding as a way of life, for it is by my weakness that I am made strong. Sometimes I find myself laboring in my own strength on something I feel You are lead-

ing me to do. I need Your peace and patience to learn how to deal with my zeal. I need to know when to let go and follow your lead. I need to let Your zeal accomplish the tasks at hand.

Respect

Job 1:21
The LORD gave, and the LORD hath taken away; blessed be the name of the LORD.
KJV

Lucy Lessons

November 20th, 2005

This morning I was in a hurry to get ready for church. I let Lucy out of the utility room where she sleeps in the winter. Our normal routine dictates that after I remove the gate, I walk to the back door to let Lucy outside. This is truth as Lucy knows it. This morning I did not follow the norm. After removing the gate, I did not walk to the back door to let her out. She bounced around enthusiastically, but perched at my feet in a confused state. She seemed to be pondering what was wrong, but she waited respectfully. I continued my tasks without much thought to Lucy's perspective.

Later in my timing, I fulfilled Lucy's expectations. What struck me was her respect in the face of my ignoring her immediate needs. She honored my delay and trusted my timing. Reverent to my position of control, she obediently awaited my decision. Lucy understands who is master as well as her role in our relationship.

Today I caught a glimpse of my role in the relationship to my master. In the Bible, Job noted, "The Lord gave and the Lord hath taken away; blessed be the name of the Lord." No matter what He decides in any situation, He deserves respect and honor. Although Jesus paid the supreme price to redeem me as his victorious bride, I would do well to remember my place in the relationship with El Elyon, God Most High. My view isn't His, and His view is superior to mine. Do I wait patiently at His feet with my emergencies? Lucy waited for me, despite her immediate need to go outside. Do I honor Him even though He is not tending to my immediate needs? Do I trust His timing when it doesn't correspond to mine? Am I reverent to His control? Today Lucy modeled for me the appropriate response. I hope to display the same respect to my loving master.

Trapped

Ps 61:1
Hear my cry, O God; Attend to my prayer.
NKJV

> Prov 3:5
> *Trust in the LORD with all your heart and lean not on your own understanding;*
> NIV

January 10th, 2006

It is 27 degrees with an 18 degree wind chill factor this morning. I had finished exercising and was headed to the shower. Lucy was agitated over an intruder at the front door, and Jim had put her outside in the cold so he could conduct business with the person at the door. I let Lucy in, but Jim wanted to leave her outside because there would be another person at the door soon, and Lucy's barking creates too much of a disturbance for Jim to conduct business.

I decided to rescue Lucy by picking her up and taking her with me. I took her behind our bedroom door, the door to the dressing room, and finally the door to the bathroom. The three doors should buffer

the noise from the front door, thereby protecting Lucy from the consequences of her barking. I turned on the bathroom heater and placed Lucy in a warm, secure location while I took a shower.

Through the frosted glass of the shower door I noticed Lucy's response. She was unaware that if she could not control her urge to bark, she would be in danger of being put back out into the cold. Her reality was that she was imprisoned behind three doors. She stood at the bathroom door and protested with her characteristic whispering, almost inaudible whine. This was her usual respectful but passionate cry.

I spoke to her through the glass and tried to reassure her that these circumstances were temporary, and if she pushed the issue, the consequences of her actions would be much worse than her current predicament. She continued in her restless state, pausing for only a moment of crouching contentment. As she paced, she pushed the inaudible protest to an audible

whine.

Lucy's response mirrored my current predicament. My mom has been trapped in her paralysis, unable to speak for close to two years now, which has been a painful experience. She was such an active, vibrant woman who loved to serve. I am caring for her now and am unable to change her circumstances, despite my constant efforts.

This is just one of several difficult situations with which I find myself right now. I feel trapped in many areas. I know God is not responsible for Mother's situation or any of the others, but I can't help questioning why, despite my cries, my circumstances do not change. I wonder if in some of the situations God has taken me in His arms and put me behind doors that are meant to protect not to trap. I wonder, if He answered my protest and opened the doors, might the consequences of my responses be much worse than my current dilemma? It is something to think about.

Unfortunately, I cannot see from God's perspective. I'm not sure if I even want that complicated view. I cannot change my circumstances; I must wait for God's timing to resolve the issues. I know He hears my cry. Perhaps I can silence my protests and spend more time in a contented posture, leaning not on my own understanding. I guess I should trust in my master more in all my circumstances.

Breath

Gen 2:7
And Jehovah God formed man of the dust of the ground, and breathed into his nostrils the breath of life; and man became a living soul.
ASV

2 Cor 12:8-10
And He said to me, "My grace is sufficient for you, for My strength is made perfect in weakness." Therefore most gladly I will rather boast in my infirmities, that the power of Christ may rest upon me. Therefore I take pleasure in infirmities, in reproaches, in needs, in persecutions, in distresses, for Christ's sake. For when I am weak, then I am strong.
NKJV

Ps 46:10
Be still, and know that I am God.
NKJV

Matt 28:20
I am with you always, even unto the end of the world.
KJV

January 10th, 2006

It was a morning like no other I could remember. A front was moving in, and the

wind was gusting. I questioned whether or not to go on my walk, but decided to go for it. My senses were bombarded with movement and sounds from the trees rustling, to the flags whipping, and the leaves flying around. Adding to the unusual sounds conjured by the wind, there were an uncharacteristic number of cars to dodge on the streets. There were more runners and dogs moving around than ever before, and as I headed down the home stretch, I felt more weathered and weary than usual.

I connected my walk with my current life status. There are more distractions in my life than ever before, and I feel bombarded by life as it crashes in on me. I feel the need to draw closer to God in the midst of this chaos.

Lucy greeted me at the door with enthusiastic anticipation of joining me on an extended walk. Unfortunately, I could not handle it today. Lucy bounced around my feet eagerly and settled down as I began to stretch on the floor. I laid on my right side with my right arm curled under my head to stretch my left quadriceps. My left hand was occupied with holding my left foot, so both hands were full. Before I knew it, Lucy crept up to my face. She normally settles just out of reach, but now she was gently moving towards me with her ears pinned pack in a humble fashion. Lucy nuzzled her nose right up to mine in a sweet attempt to smell my breath. She paused just before touching my nose to take it all in and then quietly backed away.

It occurred to me that I must draw near to God in the same manner, with a humble adoration for His very breath. His breath gave me life. I must pause to inhale His presence, drawing strength from intense closeness. I must quiet my desires for a change in my circumstances and derive inspiration from His essence. I must be still and know that He is God. His words assure me that His grace is sufficient for me, and when I am weak, He makes me strong. I am amazed that I can cuddle up to my maker, and that He is always with me. I

Lucy Lessons

love the picture of Lucy nuzzling up to me, now I want to nuzzle up to you Lord. Let me smell your very breath!

Perspective on Gifts

Jer 29:11
"For I know the plans I have for you," declares the LORD, "plans to prosper you and not to harm you, plans to give you hope and a future."
NIV

September 19th, 2006

This morning I was leaving for work when I discovered Lucy's predicament. We had workmen in our house, and because Lucy would not stop barking, she was banished to the side yard. I had left my cell phone in my bedroom, so I returned for it with my keys and purse in hand. To avoid the workmen, I chose a path that led me through the backyard. That was when I noticed that Lucy was locked in the side yard. She was not barking and seemed settled down, so I opened the gate, freeing her to roam in the whole back yard.

Lucy was ecstatic because she hates being confined to such a small, isolated area. She jumped and wiggled with excitement, and I responded to her enthusiasm by acknowledging her warmly. A few minutes later, she stood at the back door as I exited the house and tried to get through the door to come with me. As I closed the door to leave, I noticed Lucy's whimper. Later I found out from the workmen she

had protested loudly for a long time after I left. Because I had my keys and purse in hand, Lucy assumed I had released her so that she could accompany me in the car. However, it was never my intention to take her with me; I simply wanted to release her from captivity. She was so brokenhearted to find the error of her assumption. She didn't even recognize the fact that I had rescued her from spending the day isolated in the side yard.

I am reminded how different perspectives color events. I am often disappointed as I receive a gift because my expectation is not met. Instead of recognizing the gift with joy and gratitude, I am often saddened because it wasn't what I wanted. Similarly, I was frustrated with Lucy because I had done her a favor but was met with an outcry instead of gratitude.

How often does God feel the same way? How often does He rescue me from a predicament only to receive a discontented response? I must weigh changes

in my circumstances more carefully. God has an eternal perspective, and according to His word, He intends to prosper me not to harm me. I must trust His perspective in examining the events in my life. I must search for eternal perspectives before I simmer in discontentment.

Short Leash

Ps 119:105
Your word is a lamp for my feet and a light for my path.
NLT

Lucy Lessons

December 31th, 2006

After I had finished my long walk, I returned home to take Lucy on our customary shorter walk. She met me with enthusiasm and could hardly contain herself when I fetched her leash. We started out walking at a brisk pace. I require Lucy to be on the outside because she is more manageable when the smells from the yards are further away from her reach.

We made it a block or two without too much conflict when Lucy darted in front of me, almost tripping me. I reigned in her leash to maintain control, and she darted behind me quickly, almost taking us both down. I shortened her leash even more, to which she resisted. Finally after a couple more battles, I pulled her in so she had no choice but to walk right by my foot. She was on the shortest leash possible, and I held her firmly in that position. In that arrangement we were able to complete the walk without further incident.

Lucy Lessons

How often do I dart away from Holy Spirit's side when given slack? It occurred to me that I would do better with the shortest leash possible. I would stay on course better if I looked only at His feet and followed His word. The distractions that surround me are too tempting. I dart in one direction or another if given room. I must try to be content walking at His side, not anticipating the direction I think I should go, not running ahead, but staying close by His side. His word promises to light my path. I should take Him at His word.

Time of Need

Prov 12:10
A righteous man regards the life of his animal...
NKJV

May 6th, 2007

Lucy burst into the bathroom today with a little less confidence. I could tell she wanted to be near me. It reminded me of the times I allowed her to come close. She sniffed my face, and when I didn't pull away, she put her nose right under mine to breathe my breath as I exhaled. Moments like this drew us close, and I could tell she savored the scent of my breath. Today she seemed to yearn for that intimacy. She paused to let me stroke her back. There was no playfulness. Her spirit was quiet and needy as she sat at my feet. She seemed comforted by my touch and gentle speech.

In no time, Lucy struggled and lost her breakfast on the floor. She was seldom sick in her whole life, but we had recently gotten the news that she has a malignant form of melanoma. Although we removed the tumor, the tests did not give us much hope. I searched the scriptures for wisdom concerning this precious animal. Proverbs 12:10 says, "A righteous man

cares for the needs of his animal," and the King James version renders the phrase, "regardeth the life of his beast." I called Lucy my little beast and decreed blessings over her as a part of my household. I was not ready to let her go, and I didn't want to give up Lucy Lessons. In the future, when I feel closest to the Father, seemingly resonating with heaven, I will lay hands on Lucy so that she resonates as well. After all, there is no cancer in heaven!

Lucy sought my company today in her time of need. I too will pursue Your presence, my king, when I am vulnerable. I will run to your household and settle in to feel the warmth of Your touch. I hope to breathe Your breath when I am in Your presence. I hope to draw close in intimacy and I will strain my senses to move beyond the physical into the spiritual.

Anticipation

1 Chron 16:34
*Give thanks to the LORD, for he is good;
his love endures forever.*
NIV

Heb 10:19
And so, dear brothers and sisters, we can boldly enter heaven's Most Holy Place because of the blood of Jesus.
NLT

Rom 8:25
But if we hope for what we do not see, we eagerly wait for it with perseverance.
NKJV

July 13th, 2007

I returned from my walk today and began to stretch on the floor. Jim was finishing dressing by putting on his shirt. Lucy was interacting with both of us, first one and then the other. I began talking to her. Lucy usually gets to go in the car with Jim these days because Jim works from home now. Therefore, Lucy follows him closely in the mornings. However, I was talking to her, so she was responding to me as well.

Lucy Lessons

I was on the floor with Lucy, so I got a clear view of her bouncing movements. She was springing first in my direction and then in Jim's as a bird hops. It was as if her body had no weight at all because at times she looked like she was suspended in midair, floating with expectancy. When she landed, she was ready to take off in any direction depending on the slightest movement she perceived from either of us. She was responding to both of us with equal excitement. I haven't seen her move like that in a long time.

I have noticed Lucy's eager anticipation before in various situations. However, today, I considered the reason behind her behavior. Why was she so animated? I concluded that it was because of who we are to her. We are everything to her. We are her masters. She is totally dependent on us for her entire existence. She is expecting something good to come out of our interaction with her based on her previous experiences. She knows us to be good masters.

I hope to poise myself with the same anticipation, Father, for Your intentions because of who You are. You are the creator of the universe! Everything is Yours. According to Your word, You are good, and Your love endures forever. Because I have made Your son, Jesus, my lord and master, I not only have life after death, but I have access to You now. Your word says that Jesus paid the price for me to be able to enter boldly into Your presence, now! That excites me. Your word also tells me that you have plans to prosper me, not to harm me, and that I should eagerly wait for what I do not see with perseverance.

Jim grabbed his keys and Lucy raced to his side. She kept herself right at his left heel and stopped abruptly as he paused at the door. I was amazed at how she focused on his steps. She absolutely loves to go in the car.

Just as Lucy followed Jim with enthusiastic anticipation today, I want to hover in excitement for a word from You,

Father, and keenly focus my attention so closely that I take off at your heel as you move. I want to be as light as a feather, unencumbered with my agenda. I want to float weightlessly at your heel, able to halt at any moment. I want to be in step with You today, bolstered by the knowledge of who You are and that you have planned good things for me. I want to enthusiastically anticipate where we will go together.

    Later in the morning, Lucy came back from her short trip with Jim and curled up at the doorway to our bedroom. She jumped to her feet when I moved toward her. I knelt on the floor with my hands extended to her as she came to me and rolled over into my hands. I want to do the same in Your hands, Father.

Thoroughness

Prov 25:2
*It is the glory of God to conceal a matter,
But the glory of kings is to search out a matter.*
NKJV

July 16th, 2007

I was stretching on the floor after my walk today when Lucy pranced in to join me. She seemed particularly curious and began sniffing at my feet. This was not unusual behavior, so I tolerated it and imagined that she could tell where I had been by the scent. She caught my attention as she moved to one of my socks. After giving the sock a "once over," she buried her nose into it, increasing both the speed and the intensity of her smelling in one concentrated spot like a woodpecker drills a hole.

I am not sure how long Lucy spent in that one spot, but it was enough for me to laugh out loud. I asked her what she was doing, and she paused for a moment as if to contemplate my question before she began burrowing again. Amused, I let her continue as an experiment to see how long this behavior would continue.

After spending an inordinate amount of time on the one sock, Lucy re-

peated her quest on the other foot. This time she stopped and burrowed in a single spot on my shoe. After meticulously exploring that spot, she proceeded up my leg, pausing at my knee. Once again, she found a spot and tunneled into my knee. I wasn't as impressed with the fact that she was enjoying the smells as I was captivated by her zeal in exploring particular spots. It wasn't long before my patience expired, and I ended the experiment before she got much further. I'm not sure how long she would have continued, but it was longer than I had to spend.

Do I spend that much time in search of Your essence, Lord? Am I that methodical in my exploration through your Word? Do I pause to intensify my pursuit when I catch the scent of a revelation? Do I seek You with that much fervor? Your word says that it is Your glory to conceal a matter and the glory of kings to search it out. Am I passionately examining your mysteries? I was amused at Lucy's in-depth inspection. I hope to focus my efforts as thoroughly to ascertain Your essence and to discover Your word.

Devotion

Matt 6:19-21

Do not store up for yourselves treasures on earth, where moth and rust destroy, and where thieves break in and steal. But store up for yourselves treasures in heaven, where moth and rust do not destroy, and where thieves do not break in and steal. For where your treasure is, there your heart will be also.
NKJV

September 13th, 2007

Lucy was feeling good this morning, following both Jim and me around with an enthusiastic prance. At times, she paused to look intently at me, peering into my eyes. She moved about simultaneously in her world and in mine. Using her finest sense, she sniffed Jim's shoes to gather information about where he had been. Applying her best skill, she rolled over to engage both Jim and me in a connection. We both lovingly rubbed her belly.

Earlier that morning, I had read the verse in Matthew concerning storing up treasures in heaven and was contemplating what types of treasures existed there. Previously I had skimmed over that verse, but today I allowed my imagination to dwell on treasures in heaven. What type of treasures could we store up in heaven? Would they be tangible or intangible? I remembered thinking about "rest" being passed out like my mother's dinner rolls, so it was a natural transition for me to wonder about

other heavenly commodities such as honor or wisdom. What would a bucket of honor look like? If our natural bodies transform into supernatural ones in heaven, do intangible commodities convert to concrete ones?

After drifting in thought along these lines, I turned back to Lucy and addressed her as I prepared to leave for work. In her typical fashion, she was doing her best to understand and cooperate with my words. Then it hit me. What Lucy gave us without measure was her devotion. It was all she had to give, but she gave us loads of it. But what if devotion were a real essence in heavenly places? What if it were an article of trade in the spiritual realm? What if we gave full credibility to generating the intangible as we do in producing the tangible? How would that affect our eternal position? It was something to think about.

Stumbling

James 3:2
For we all stumble in many things.
NKJV

Lucy Lessons

November 11th, 2011

Lucy was in the back yard with her coat on today. It was a warm, sunny, November day, and she was taking advantage of being outside. It has been four years since Lucy's melanoma diagnosis, but she has been doing relatively well. I changed her diet to an "all-natural one" and have been careful not to give her human food. There have been no cancer reoccurrences, and until today she seemed to be prospering.

I was baking cookies in the kitchen when I heard Lucy yelp. It was a piercing, desperate cry for help. I ran to the window to see Lucy struggling to stay afloat in the pool. I screamed for Jim and we both ran outside to save her. After Jim fetched her from the water and removed her wet coat, I bundled her in a blanket and held her until we both quit shivering. That took quite a while.

Both Jim and I hovered over Lucy

Lucy Lessons

as we unwrapped her and put her down to survey the damage. Her hind legs gave out as she took the first step. My heart broke at the sight, and Jim reassured me that she would probably get better with time. I picked her up again and put her in her bed for a nap.

Lately, Lucy has been drifting to one side as she walks, so Jim and I surmised that is what she did when she fell into the pool. We discussed how we would handle this in the future, and Jim decided to cover the pool in the winter and line the edge of the pool with the water bags that hold our pool cover in place in warm weather. Neither of us could bear a repeat of this traumatic event.

Your word, God, tells me that we all stumble in many things. Oh how Your heart must ache when we do! I have a new mental picture of that as I am still quivering over the sight of Lucy struggling in that water. She was flailing far from the steps, struggling with the weight of her coat, and

Lucy Lessons

I can't even bear the thought of what one more minute would have meant. Later that day, Lucy regained some of her bounce. She was able to walk with only an occasional drift to one side. I was amazed at her resilience. Mine was slower coming. I am not sure I can put into words how I feel, God. Thank you for enduring my stumblings with such love and grace. I am glad You are God and I am not.

Epilogue

God was gracious to give Lucy eight months after she fell in the pool that November day. He heard my prayers. I can't help but associate Lucy in her final days with my mom in hers. Mother was vibrant as she aged, as was Lucy. Neither of them looked their age, and both seemed to approach this stage energetically, ignoring the apparent signs of aging. There were physical nuisances that required medication, but these hindrances were taken in stride. Tragically, mother suffered a debilitating stroke, which robbed her of her speech and her independence. She was unable to communicate her feelings, and in her last days, she inexplicably refused her medications at times.

Lucy was not the same after she fell

into the pool. In her last months she periodically lost the mobility in her hind legs, and I knew her days were short. She seemed to be in some pain, so we gave her medications to address her discomfort. In the last days, it grieved my heart to see Lucy exhibiting the same inexplicable reluctance in refusing her medications as my mom did with hers.

I can only imagine how my Father must feel as He looks on His children when they become old and frail, stumbling as they move about. My heart broke in my inability to stop the inevitable. Lucy seemed restless as she staggered around and kept close to me. I felt helpless in assisting her face this part of life. I held her to comfort her, and as she nestled down to rest in my arms, my heart ached knowing these times were preciously short.

This is probably where my Lucy Lessons cease to provide insight into how the Father must feel. Unlike me, the Father knows what is ahead and must look for-

Lucy Lessons

ward to more intimacy with His own children when they leave the distractions of life and come home to be with Him. He must look sweetly on the frailty and dependency of old age, knowing that soon the faithful servants who call upon His name will be given a new body to replace the worn-out, failing one. He has eternity to fellowship with us, and I know this perpetual relationship must be a part of His everlasting plan.

Two years after Mother went to be with the Lord, Lucy fell in the pool one last time. I miss them both.

I was blessed with a precious pet for over 17 years. I was Lucy's master, and she was my faithful companion dependent on my provision. Although she was clueless to my world, she enhanced it greatly. I delighted in so many things about her, including her excitement to see me and her devotion to following my every movement. I loved the way she peered up at me through her eyebrows and relished smelling my breath.

It tickled me when she reluctantly obeyed, and it brought me joy when I watched her savor the wind in her face. Lucy made me laugh as well as think. On a regular basis, she helped me consider the sacrifice Jesus made to establish a relationship with me and exchange His life for mine. Lucy's behavior made me contemplate and question mine. Her relationship with me helped me to refine my relationship with my master. For that I am eternally grateful.

Lucy Lessons

Don't Look At Me

1 John 2:20
*But you have an anointing from the Holy
One, and you know all things.
NKJV*

By Sarah Stratton

When Nancy approached me about doing drawings for Lucy Lessons I thought, "Sure, this should be no problem. I can whip those suckers out in no time." I expected it to be a fun project with little challenge. After all, this was nothing I hadn't done before – or so I thought.

As a kid in school I would sit and sketch dogs and various other things. I had many different styles: cartoon, portrait, abstract, etc. It was quick, easy, painless, and when it was time to move on to the next class, I would pack up my books and sketches, and they would not be seen or thought of much again.

Lucy Lessons was different.

When I started this project, I realized I had begun a journey that was glorious and stretching but felt like it was mostly uphill. These quick drawings that I thought I could "whip out'" somehow stretched out to almost a year. Believe me, it wasn't because I was slacking off, either.

As I approached the project, I tried to work on the drawings in order. I would read the story and then mull it over for a couple days. I would picture Lucy acting the story out, the emotions in her ears and eyebrows, and what position she would have been in. Some came quick and easy and some were rough. I tended to skip the hardest ones with the intent to return to them at a later date. A couple in particular presented the greatest difficulty.

I had trouble with *"Whoof"* mostly because I have had trouble drawing hands and feet in the past. I kept putting the chapter off until I finally reached the point where I had gotten most of the drawings done, and I needed to go ahead and push through. I had my husband, Brian, stand in front of me with his hands as if they were around Lucy's snout so I could get the positioning right. It worked out, but the time to celebrate was short, for now it was time

to attack the chapter titled *"Vulnerability."*

I treated this one as if it were the plague. I tip-toed and danced around it, postponing it time after time. When I finally did try to work on it, I never felt satisfied by what I had done. Each time, I would labor over the sketch, willing it to come together. Each time, it would be all wrong. One night, I decided I was not going to bed until I finally finished it. It was not my favorite drawing, but I convinced myself it would work.

It was wonderful to get to call Nancy to tell her I had indeed completed the drawings. The next week we met to discuss what I had sent her, and she said she loved them all! Not only that, but everyone she showed them to loved them as well, except for one problem: they didn't quite see "it" in the "Vulnerability" sketch. Despite the disappointment I felt, I knew Nancy was right.

A few days later I had a meeting

scheduled with my pastor at church. I brought my drawings to show her because it was quite a large part of my life at that point. The drawings, and especially "Vulnerability," had been at the forefront of my mind at all times, and I was becoming quite a mess. My pastor flipped through the pictures one by one and giggled at Lucy and all her antics. Suddenly, as I was looking through the pages with her, I blurted out, "I'm having trouble with vulnerability."

She simply looked at me and raised her eyebrows as if saying, "Ya think?" Struck by the irony of what just happened, we laughed and laughed. After that revelation, there was literally nothing left to be spoken, and I couldn't have said it more plainly if I tried. Thank you Holy Spirit.

All my life I've been an artist at heart, but I never intended for anyone to see my work. It was a very tender part of me that I held very close. Just like my sketches I would draw in school, I would pour out my heart on paper but never share it. It was as

if I were saying, "Don't look at this part of me."

My pastor was so wise to point out that in hiding my artwork I wasn't valuing or honoring the gift God created in me. It is a gift He gave me to glorify Him, and I thought it wasn't as special or useful as other gifts my friends or family had. Through this experience, the name of the "Vulnerability" passage became reality in my life.

Working on *Lucy Lessons* was different from any other artwork I had ever created. This time, the point was for others to see. As a result, I found that the drawings that were related to topics in which I didn't struggle were simple and quick and I didn't have to dig very deep. But on the ones that touched me personally, I had to learn to open up a part of me that I had never allowed anyone to see before. I had to pour my heart out on paper and lay it out bare for the world to examine. This shook me deeply, but God's grace saw me through.

I got new revelation on the part of the song that says, "Hide it under a bushel, NO! I'm gonna let it shine." Just as Nancy had to be vulnerable with her words, I had to get deep and vulnerable with my lines and shapes. I humbled myself before the Lord and said, "Not my will, Lord, but your will be done. I repent for building walls around my heart and trying not to stick out. I'm so sorry for not honoring the gifts you gave me and I do thank you for them. I will use them to glorify you. Please tear down this wall and help me be vulnerable."

These completed drawings are proof that He heard me and healed me. After looking back at the drawings, I noticed that some of them are inconsistent with Lucy's look. However, I purposely refrained from "fixing" them. For me, flipping through these pictures is similar to flipping through a journal documenting a difficult but triumphant journey. It may have been hard, but God used this time to grow me, and I wouldn't change it. Now, rather than saying, "Don't look at me!" I get to say, "Look

who the Lord created me to be and look at what He is saying through me!"

I encourage anyone reading this to face the journey ahead. Do not try to take the easy way. Sometimes it is uphill most of the way, but the Lord is taking us deeper and getting rid of any crutch that we may be holding on to that is holding us back. It is worth it. He really is that good.

Lucy Lessons

www.ingramcontent.com/pod-product-compliance
Lightning Source LLC
Chambersburg PA
CBHW071849090426
42811CB00004B/534